Knit
LONDON

10 ICONIC LONDON PROJECTS

Emma King

COLLINS & BROWN

First published in the United Kingdom
in 2012
by Collins & Brown
10 Southcombe Street
London
W14 0RA

An imprint of Anova Books Company Ltd

Copyright © Collins & Brown 2012
Text and pattern/project copyright
© Emma King 2012

Photography by Holly Jolliffe
Illustrations by Marcus Butt

Distributed in the United States and Canada
by Sterling Publishing Co, 387 Park Avenue
South, New York, NY 10016-8810, USA

ISBN 978-1-90844-908-5

A CIP catalogue record for this book is
available from the British Library.

10 9 8 7 6 5 4 3 2 1

Reproduction by Mission Productions,
Hong Kong
Printed and bound by Everbest Printing, China

This book can be ordered direct from the
publisher at www.anovabooks.com

CONTENTS

LONDON CALLING!

Join us in a knitted celebration of London's world-famous landmarks. Deciding which project to knit first will be as difficult as deciding how to spend a day's sightseeing in London!

First choose your mode of transport, and this is a tricky one… Will you hop on a classic red Routemaster bus or hail a black cab?

Next admire the fantastic architecture that makes up the iconic London skyline. Old favourites such as Big Ben and Tower Bridge sit happily alongside popular newcomers like the Gherkin and the London Eye.

Make a quick call home from a red phone box then try to make one of the Queen's Guards laugh by waving your Union Jack flag (knitted of course!) at the Changing the Guard ceremony.

There's a lot to learn about London's history, so we have included fun facts and figures to keep you entertained as you knit.

What are you waiting for?

Knit London!

ROUTEMASTER BUS

MEASUREMENTS
Height: 17cm (6¾in)
Depth: 11cm (4¼in)
Length: 20cm (8in)

YARN
One 100g (210m/230yd) ball
of Patons Cotton DK
in each of Red 2115 (A)
and Black 2712 (B);
One 50g (115m/126yd)
ball of Rowan Cashsoft DK
in Mist 505 (C)

MATERIALS
One pair of 3.25mm (US 3)
knitting needles;
Tapestry needle;
Four cardboard discs, each
approx. 4cm (1½in) diameter;
Foam and wadding (batting);
Two 15mm (⅝in) silver
cover buttons

TENSION (GAUGE)
25 stitches and 34 rows to
10cm (4in) over stocking
(stockinette) stitch using
3.25mm (US 3) needles.

ABBREVIATIONS
See pages 94–95 for
abbreviations and information
on charts, the intarsia technique
and wrap stitch.

The classic Routemaster
bus still runs on two
heritage routes. Route 9
goes between Trafalgar
Square and Kensington
High Street and route 15
between Trafalgar Square
and Tower Hill.

DRIVER'S SIDE

Using A, cast on 49 sts.
Work all 49 rows of the driver's side chart provided, beginning with a knit row and working in stocking (stockinette) stitch (knit on RS, purl on WS) unless indicated otherwise. Change colours using the intarsia technique and shape the top as indicated. When completed, cast (bind) off.

PASSENGERS' SIDE

Cast on 49 sts as follows:
42 sts using A, 3 sts using B, 1 st using C, 3 sts using B.
Work as for the driver's side but follow the passengers' side chart instead. When completed, cast (bind) off.

FRONT

Cast on 21 sts as follows:
7 sts using A, 1 st using C, 6 sts using B, 1 st using C, 6 sts using A.
Work all 49 rows of the front chart provided, beginning with a knit row and working in stocking (stockinette) stitch (knit on RS, purl on WS) unless indicated otherwise. Note that the radiator grill is worked in garter stitch. Change colours using the intarsia technique and shape the top as indicated. When completed, cast (bind) off.

BACK

Cast on 21 sts as follows:
5 sts using B, 16 st using A.
Work as for the front but follow the back chart instead. When completed, cast (bind) off.

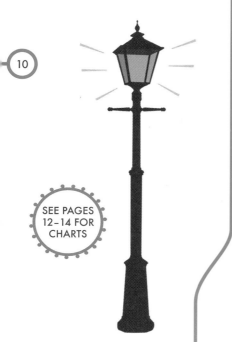

10

SEE PAGES 12–14 FOR CHARTS

ROOF

Using A, cast on 21 sts.
Row 1 (RS): Knit.
Row 2: Purl.
Repeat last two rows until work
measures 18cm (7in) from
cast-on edge.
Cast (bind) off.

BASE

Using B, cast on 21 sts.
Row 1 (RS): Knit.
Row 2: Purl.
Repeat last two rows until work
measures 18cm (7in) from
cast-on edge.
Cast (bind) off.

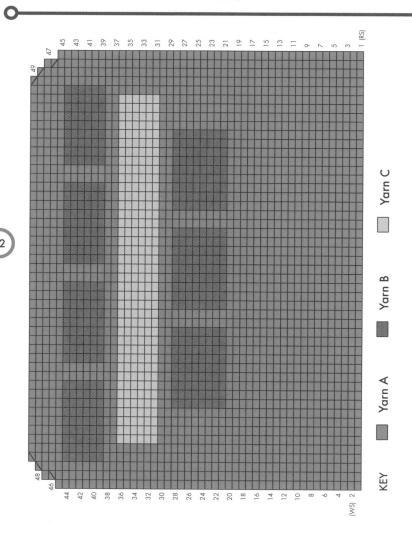

(12)

KEY ░ Yarn A ▓ Yarn B ▒ Yarn C

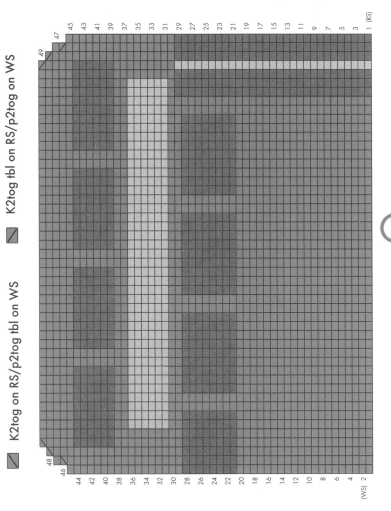

K2tog tbl on RS/p2tog on WS

K2tog on RS/p2tog tbl on WS

13

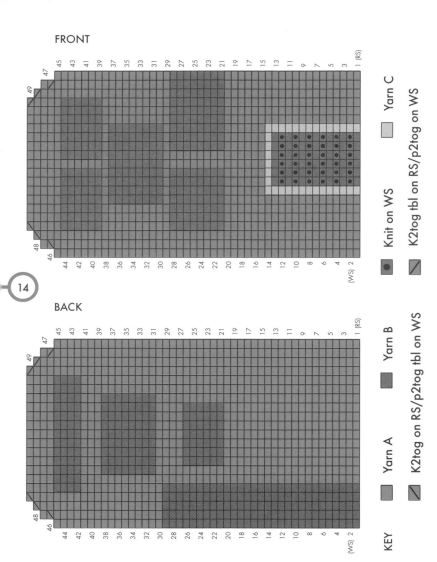

FRONT

14

BACK

KEY

Yarn A   Yarn B   Yarn C

Knit on WS

● K2tog on RS/p2tog tbl on WS

◢ K2tog tbl on RS/p2tog on WS

WHEELS (make 4)
Using B, cast on 9 sts.
Row 1 (RS): Knit.
Next row: *P6, wrap st, turn, knit to end.
Repeat from * until a circle has formed.
Cast (bind) off.
The knitted piece will naturally curl into a tyre shape. Encourage it to do so, sewing along the cast-on edge. You will now have a circular piece of knitting that curls in at the edges. Insert a cardboard disc into the knitted circle, using the curling edges to trap the disc inside. Then run a piece of yarn B all the way around the edge of the circle (a running stitch) and pull the two ends together – this will act like a drawstring and pull the knitted circle together, covering the disc. Fasten securely, leaving an end to sew the wheel to the bus.

FINISHING
Using mattress stitch and the photographs as a guide, sew the four sides of the bus together, matching windows and doors where necessary. Sew the roof onto the bus. Cut foam to fit inside the bus, and add wadding (batting) around the foam to accentuate the bus's curved shape. Sew on the base and then all four wheels. Sew the silver cover buttons to the front of the bus on either side of the radiator grill for headlights. Using yarn C, embroider the number and destination.

An updated version of the iconic doubledecker Routemaster bus will be launched in 2012.

BLACK CAB

MEASUREMENTS
Height: 14cm (5½in)
Depth: 11cm (4¼in)
Length: 24cm (9½in)

YARN
Two 100g (210m/230yd) balls
of Patons Cotton DK
in Black 2712 (A);
One 50g (115m/126yd) ball
of Rowan Cashsoft DK
in Blink 534 (B);
One 50g (140m/153yd)
ball of Rowan Siena 4ply
in Frost 653 (C);
Small amount of Patons Fab
in Canary 2305 (D);
Small amounts of Rowan
Handknit Cotton in Florence
350 (E) and Bleached 263 (F)

TENSION (GAUGE)
25 stitches and 34 rows to
10cm (4in) over stocking
(stockinette) stitch using
3.25mm (US 3) needles.

MATERIALS
One pair of 3.25mm (US 3)
knitting needles;
Two 3.25mm (US 3)
double-pointed needles;
Two stitch markers;
Tapestry needle;
Four cardboard discs,
approx. 4cm (1½in) diameter;
Foam and wadding (batting);
Two 15mm (⅝in) silver
cover buttons

ABBREVIATIONS
See pages 94–95 for
abbreviations and information
on charts, the intarsia technique
and wrap stitch.

PASSENGERS' SIDE

Using 3.25mm (US 3) needles and A, cast on 61 sts.

Row 1 (RS): K19, [p1, k13] three times.

Row 2: P13, [k1, p13] twice, k1, p19.

Row 3: K2tog, k17, [p1, k13] twice, p1, k to last st, m1, k1.

Row 4: P14, [k1, p13] twice, k1, p18.

Row 5: K18, [p1, k13] twice, p1, k14.

Row 6: P14, [k1, p13] twice, k1, p18.

Row 7: K2tog, k16, [p1, k13] twice, p1, k to last st, m1, k1.

Row 8: P15, [k1, p13] twice, k1, p17.

Row 9: K17, [p1, k13] twice, p1, k15.

Row 10: P15, [k1, p13] twice, k1, p17.

Row 11: K2tog, k15, [p1, k13] twice, p1, k to last st, m1, k1.

Row 12: P16, [k1, p13] twice, k1, p16.

Row 13: K16, [p1, k13] twice, p1, k16.

Row 14: P16, [k1, p13] twice, k1, p16.

Row 15: K2tog, k14, [p1, k13] twice, p1, k to last st, m1, k1.

Row 16: P17, [k1, p13] twice, k1, p15.

Row 17: K15, [p1, k13] twice, p1, k17.

Row 18: P17, [k1, p13] twice, k1, p15.

Row 19: K15, [p1, k13] twice, p1, k to last st, m1, k1. (62 sts)

Row 20: P18, [k1, p13] twice, k1, p15.

Row 21: K15, [p1, k13] twice, p1, k18.

Row 22: P18, [k1, p13] twice, k1, p15.

Repeat last two rows once more.

Row 25: Cast (bind) off 2 sts, k13 (includes st used to cast (bind) off), p1, [k13, p1] twice, k18. (60 sts)

Row 26: Cast (bind) off 16 sts, p2 (includes st used to cast (bind) off), [k1, p13] twice, k1, p to last 2 sts, p2tog. (43 sts)

Work rows 27–43 from the passengers' side chart provided, beginning with a knit row and working in stocking (stockinette) stitch (knit on RS, purl on WS) unless indicated otherwise. Change colours using the intarsia technique and shape

SEE PAGE 21 FOR CHART

the outer edges of the front
and rear windows as indicated.
When completed, continue
using A only as follows:
Row 44: Purl.
Row 45: Knit.
Row 46: P2tog, p to last 2 sts,
p2tog. (41 sts)
Row 47: K2tog, k to last 2 sts,
k2tog. (39 sts)
Cast (bind) off.

DRIVER'S SIDE
Using 3.25mm (US 3) needles
and A, cast on 61 sts.
Row 1 (RS): K13, [p1, k13]
twice, p1, k19.
Row 2: P19, [k1, p13] three
times.
Row 3: K1, m1, k12, [p1, k13]
twice, p1, k to last 2 sts, k2tog.
Row 4: P18, [k1, p13] twice,
k1, p14.
Row 5: K14, [p1, k13] twice,
p1, k18.
Row 6: P18, [k1, p13] twice,
k1, p14.
Row 7: K1, m1, [k13, p1] three
times, k to last 2 sts, k2tog.
Row 8: P17, [k1, p13] twice,
k1, p15.
Row 9: K15, [p1, k13] twice,
p1, k17.

Row 10: P17, [k1, p13] twice,
k1, p15.
Row 11: K1, m1, k14,
[p1, k13] twice, p1, k to last
2 sts, k2tog.
Row 12: P16, [k1, p13] twice,
k1, p16.
Row 13: K16, [p1, k13] twice,
p1, k16.
Row 14: P16, [k1, p13] twice,
k1, p16.
Row 15: K1, m1, k15,
[p1, k13] twice, p1, k to last
2 sts, k2tog.
Row 16: P15, [k1, p13] twice,
k1, p17.
Row 17: K17, [p1, k13] twice,
p1, k15.
Row 18: P15, [k1, p13] twice,
k1, p17.
Row 19: K1, m1, k16,
[p1, k13] twice, p1, k15.
(62 sts)
Row 20: P15, [k1, p13] twice,
k1, p18.
Row 21: K18, [p1, k13] twice,
p1, k15.
Row 22: P15, [k1, p13] twice,
k1, p18.
Repeat last two rows once more.
Row 25: Cast (bind) off 16 sts,
k2 (includes st used to cast (bind)
off), [p1, k13] twice, p1, k to last
2 sts, k2tog. (45 sts)

Row 26: Cast (bind) off 2 sts, p12 (includes st used to cast (bind) off), [k1, p13] twice, k1, p2. (43 sts)
Work rows 27–43 from the driver's side chart provided, beginning with a knit row and working in stocking (stockinette) stitch (knit on RS, purl on WS) unless indicated otherwise. Change colours using the intarsia technique and shape the outer edges of the front and rear windows as indicated. When completed, continue using A only as follows:
Row 44: Purl.

Row 45: Knit.
Row 46: P2tog, p to last 2 sts, p2tog. (41 sts)
Row 47: K2tog, k to last 2 sts, k2tog. (39 sts)
Cast (bind) off.

Black cab drivers must pass 'The Knowledge', a test to prove their knowledge of London's streets and landmarks.

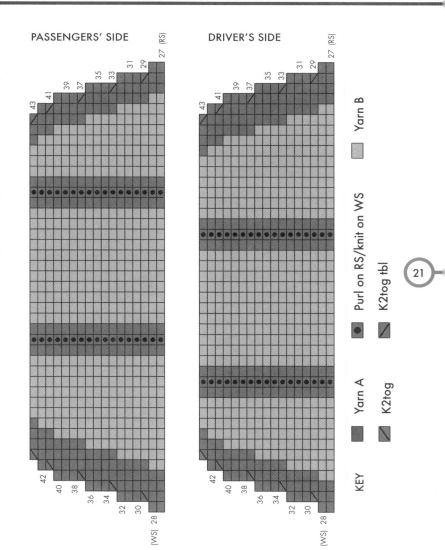

PASSENGERS' SIDE

DRIVER'S SIDE

27 (RS)

29

31

33

35

37

39

41

43

42

40

38

36

34

32

30

28 (WS)

KEY

Yarn A

Yarn B

Purl on RS/knit on WS

K2tog

K2tog tbl

21

BONNET

Top of Bonnet and Radiator

Using 3.25mm (US 3) needles and A, cast on 27 sts.
Row 1 (RS): Knit.
Row 2: Purl.
Row 3: K2tog, k to last 2 sts, k2tog. (25 sts)
Row 4: Purl.
Row 5: Knit.
Row 6: Purl.
Row 7: K2tog, k to last 2 sts, k2tog. (23 sts)
Row 8: Purl.
Row 9: K2tog, k to last 2 sts, k2tog. (21 sts)
Repeat last two rows twice more. (17 sts)
Row 14: Purl.
Row 15: Knit.
Row 16: Purl.

Row 17: K2tog, k to last 2 sts, k2tog. (15 sts)
Row 18: Purl.
Row 19: Knit.
Row 20: Purl.
Row 21: Knit.
Row 22: Knit (this creates a ridge).
Work rows 23–39 from the radiator chart provided, beginning with a knit row and working in stocking (stockinette) stitch (knit on RS, purl on WS) unless indicated otherwise. Change colours using the intarsia technique. When completed, continue using A only as follows:
Row 40: Purl.
Row 41: Knit.
Row 42: Purl.
Repeat last two rows once more. Cast (bind) off.

RADIATOR

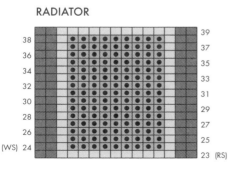

38 37
36 35
34 33
32 31
30 29
28 27
26 25
(WS) 24 23 (RS)

KEY

Yarn A

Yarn B

● Purl on RS/ knit on WS

Yarn C

Passengers' Side of Bonnet

Using 3.25mm (US 3) needles and A and with RS facing, pick up and knit 18 sts along side of bonnet, starting at ridge at top of radiator and working up to start of windscreen.

Row 1 (WS): Purl.
Row 2: Knit.
Row 3: Purl.
Repeat last two rows ten more times.
Cast (bind) off.

Driver's Side of Bonnet

Work as for passengers' side of bonnet, picking up from the windscreen down to the ridge at top of radiator.

HEADLIGHT PANELS
Passengers' Side

Using 3.25mm (US 3) needles and A, cast on 11 sts.
Row 1 (RS): K6, sl1, k4.
Row 2: Purl.
Repeat last two rows nine more times.
Row 21: K6, sl1, k4.
Row 22: Cast (bind) off 4 sts, p to end. (7 sts)
Row 23: Knit.
Row 24: Purl.
Row 25: Knit.
Repeat last two rows twice more.

Row 30: Purl.
Row 31: K to last 2 sts, k2tog. (6 sts)
Row 32: Purl.
Row 33: Knit.
Row 34: Purl.
Row 35: K to last 2 sts, k2tog. (5 sts)
Repeat rows 32–35 twice more. (3 sts)
Row 44: Purl.
Row 45: K1, k2tog. (2 sts)
Cast (bind) off.

Driver's Side

Using 3.25mm (US 3) needles and A, cast on 11 sts.
Row 1 (RS): K4, sl1, k6.
Row 2: Purl.
Repeat last two rows ten more times.
Row 23: Cast (bind) off 4 sts, k to end. (7 sts)
Row 24: Purl.
Row 25: Knit.
Row 26: Purl.
Repeat last two rows twice more.
Row 31: K2tog, k to end. (6 sts)
Rows 32–34: As rows 24–26.
Row 35: K2tog, k to end. (5 sts)
Repeat rows 32–35 twice more. (3 sts)
Row 44: Purl.
Row 45: K2tog, k1. (2 sts)
Cast (bind) off.

WINDSCREEN, ROOF AND REAR (worked all in one piece)

Using 3.25mm (US 3) needles and B and with RS facing, pick up and knit 27 sts along cast-on edge of bonnet.

Row 1 (WS): Purl.
Row 2: Knit.
Row 3: Purl.

Repeat last two rows seven more times.

Change to A.

Row 18: Knit.
Row 19: Purl.

Repeat last two rows until work measures 11cm (4¼in) from row 18, ending with a WS row. Place a marker at each end of last row.

Next row (RS): Knit.
Next row: Purl.

Repeat last two rows twice more. Work the next ten rows from the rear window chart provided, working the chart in the usual way. When completed, continue using A only as follows:

Next row (RS): Knit.
Next row: Purl.

Repeat last two rows twice more.

Next row: Purl (this creates a ridge).

Next row: Purl.
Next row: Knit.

Repeat last two rows four more times.

Next row: P8, k11, p8.

Work the next three rows from the rear registration plate chart provided, working the chart in the usual way. When completed, continue using A only as follows:

Next row (WS): P8, k1, p9, k1, p8.
Next row: K8, p11, k8.
Next row: Purl.
Next row: Knit.
Next row: Purl.

Repeat last two rows three more times.

Cast (bind) off.

FRONT REGISTRATION PLATE

Using 3.25mm (US 3) needles and F, cast on 11 sts.

Row 1 (RS): Knit.
Row 2: Purl.

Repeat last two rows once more.

Cast (bind) off.

BASE

Using 3.25mm (US 3) needles and A, cast on 27 sts.

Row 1 (RS): Knit.
Row 2: Purl.

Repeat last two rows until work measures 24cm (9½in) from cast-on edge.

Cast (bind) off.

REAR WINDOW

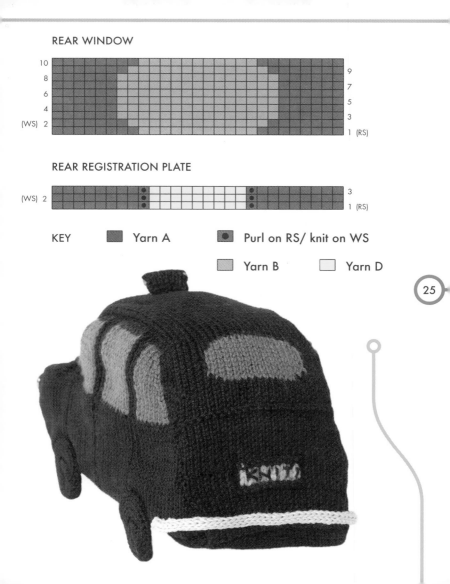

10
8
6
4
(WS) 2

9
7
5
3
1 (RS)

REAR REGISTRATION PLATE

(WS) 2

3
1 (RS)

KEY
■ Yarn A
● Purl on RS/ knit on WS

■ Yarn B
□ Yarn D

25

WHEELS (make 4)
Using 3.25mm (US 3) needles and A, cast on 9 sts.
Row 1 (RS): Knit.
Next row: *P6, wrap st, turn, k to end.
Repeat from * until a circle has formed, then cast (bind) off. The knitted piece will naturally curl into a tyre shape. Encourage it to do so, sewing along the cast-on edge. You will now have a circular piece of knitting that curls in at the edges. Insert a cardboard disc into the knitted circle, using the curling edges to trap the disc inside. Then run a piece of yarn A all the way around the edge of the circle (a running stitch) and pull the two ends together – this will act like a drawstring and pull the knitted circle together, covering the disc. Fasten securely, leaving an end to sew the wheel to the taxi.

BUMPERS (make 2)
Each bumper is made from an i-cord as follows:
Using 3.25mm (US 3) double-pointed needles and C, cast on 4 sts.
Row 1 (RS): Knit.
You would now usually turn the needles to work the next row, but to make an i-cord DO NOT TURN. Instead, slide the stitches to the other end of the double-pointed needle, ready to be knitted again. The yarn will now be at the left edge of the knitting, and so to knit the next row you must pull the yarn tightly across the back of the work and then knit one more row. Continue in this way, never turning and always sliding the work to the other end of the double-pointed needle. The right side of the work will always be facing you. Repeat row 1 until cord measures 16cm (6¼in).
Break off yarn, thread through stitches and pull together.

TAXI SIGN
Using 3.25mm (US 3) needles and E, cast on 9 sts.
Row 1 (RS): Knit.
Row 2: Purl.
Repeat last two rows once more.
Change to A.
Row 5: Knit.
Row 6: Knit (this creates a ridge).
Row 7: Knit.
Row 8: Purl.
Repeat last two rows once more.
Cast (bind) off.

FINISHING

Using mattress stitch and the photographs as a guide, sew both side panels to the windscreen/roof/rear section, starting at the base of the windscreen and ending at the rear bumper. Sew the base into position, along one side, across the back and along the other side, leaving the front seam open. Cut foam to fit inside the base of the cab, shaping it to fit inside the bonnet, all the way to the rear bumper and up to the height of the doors. Insert wadding (batting) above the foam, accentuating the classic shape of the London cab.

Close the bonnet and make sure that the bonnet sides are tucked straight down. The wings of the cab will be hanging free at the moment, apart from the cast-on edge that you have sewn to the base of the cab. Sew the cast-off (bound-off) edge of the bonnet (bottom of radiator) to the base of the cab.

Join the passengers' headlight panel to the passengers' side wing, and the driver's headlight panel to the driver's side wing as follows, noting that the wider section of each headlight panel (where you k6) will form the front of the taxi where the headlight will sit and the k4 folds in to meet the bonnet side. With RS facing, sew the edge of the headlight panel to the front edge of the side panel and then along the edge of the side panel where you cast (bound) off 16 sts. Insert wadding (batting) into the wing and then slipstitch the other side of the headlight panel to the bonnet side, working about 7mm (¼in) back from the radiator and below the edge of the bonnet – this will help to create the classic bonnet shape. Do the same for the other side.

Sew the wheels to the cab, positioning them where the wings meet the doors. Sew the bumpers to the front and back of the cab. Using yarn A, embroider 'TAXI' onto the front of the taxi sign. Fold the sign in half at the ridge and neatly sew around the edges. Sew the taxi sign to the centre front of the roof. Using yarn A, embroider 'KNIT 1' onto the front and rear registration plates, then sew them to the front and rear of the cab. Sew the silver cover buttons to the front of the cab at the top middle of the headlight panels.

STREET SIGN

SEE PAGES 30-33 FOR CHARTS

MEASUREMENTS
Height: 24cm (9½in)
Width: 31cm (12¼in)

YARN
One 50g (115m/126yd) ball of Rowan Siena 4ply in each of White 651 (A), Chilli 666 (B) and Black 674 (C), plus extra for back of cushion (optional)

MATERIALS
One pair of 3mm (US 2/3) knitting needles; Cushion filling; Sew-on velcro strips, approx 31cm (12¼in); Tapestry needle

TENSION (GAUGE)
28 stitches and 38 rows to 10cm (4in) over stocking (stockinette) stitch using 3mm (US 2/3) needles.

ABBREVIATIONS
See pages 94–95 for abbreviations and information on charts and the intarsia technique.

CUSHION FRONT
Using A, cast on 87 sts. Beginning with a knit row, work in stocking (stockinette) stitch (knit on RS, purl on WS) from the sign chart provided, changing colours using the intarsia technique as indicated. Refer to the alphabet chart if you wish to insert different street names of your choice. When all 88 rows of the chart have been completed, cast (bind) off.

CUSHION BACK
Lower back
Using A, cast on 87 sts.
Row 1 (RS): Knit.
Row 2: Purl.
Repeat last two rows until 64 rows have been completed.
Row 65: K3 (p3, k3) to end.
Row 66: P3 (k3, p3) to end.
Repeat last two rows three more times.
Cast (bind) off in pattern.

28

Upper back

Using A, cast on 87 sts.
Row 1: K3 (p3, k3) to end.
Row 2: P3 (k3, p3) to end.
Repeat last two rows three more times.
Row 9: Knit.
Row 10: Purl.
Repeat last two rows eight more times.
Cast (bind) off.

FINISHING

Using mattress stitch and with RS facing, join the cast-on edge of the lower back to the cast-on edge of the cushion front and then join the side seams. In the same way, join the cast-off (bound-off) edge of the upper back to the cast-off (bound-off) edge of the cushion front and then join the side seams. The ribs should overlap. Insert cushion filling and sew a strip of velcro on each side of the overlap to keep the cushion closed.

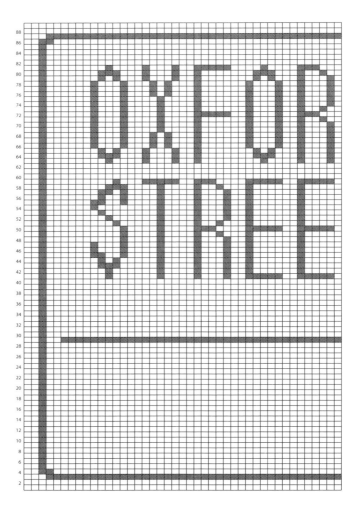

The chart has been divided where the pages of the book join.
Work across both sections as if they were a single chart.

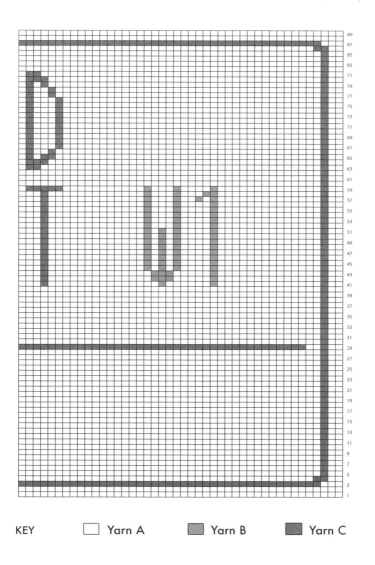

KEY   ☐ Yarn A   ▨ Yarn B   ▨ Yarn C

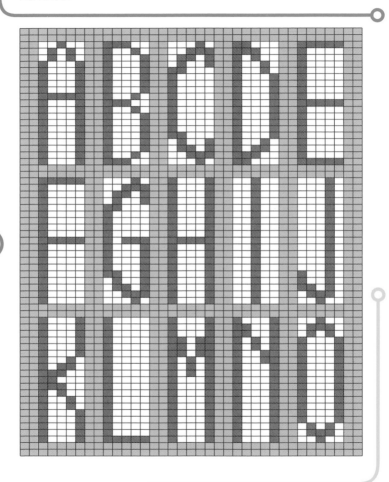

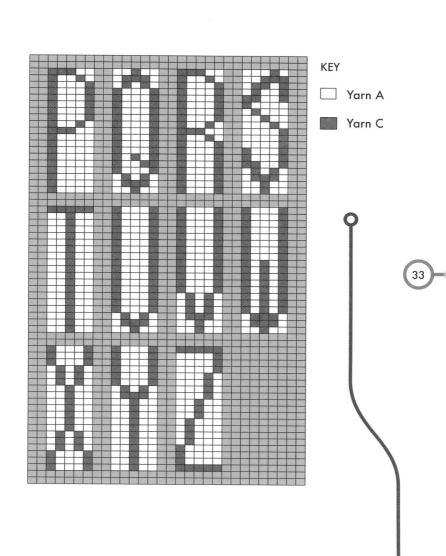

KEY

☐ Yarn A

■ Yarn C

TELEPHONE BOX

MEASUREMENTS
Height: 23cm (9in)
Depth: 9cm (3½in)

YARN
One 50g (115m/126yd) ball of
Rowan Cotton Glacé in each of
Poppy 741 (A), Black 727 (B)
and Bleached 726 (C)

MATERIALS
One pair of 3mm (US 2/3)
knitting needles;
Tapestry needle;
Foam and wadding (batting)

TENSION (GAUGE)
25 stitches and 36 rows to
10cm (4in) over stocking
(stockinette) stitch using
3mm (US 2/3) needles.

ABBREVIATIONS
See pages 94–95 for
abbreviations and information
on charts, the intarsia technique
and wrap stitch.

The prototype for the
iconic red telephone box
is in the entrance arch to
the Royal Academy of
Arts on Piccadilly.

SIDES (make 3)
Using A, cast on 25 sts.
Row 1 (RS): K4, p1, k15, p1, k4.
Row 2: P4, k1, p15, k1, p4.
Row 3: K4, p1, k15, p1, k4.
Row 4: P4, k1, p2, k11, p2, k1, p4.
Row 5: K4, p1, k2, p1, k9, p1, k2, p1, k4.
Row 6: P4, k1, p2, k1, p9, k1, p2, k1, p4.
Row 7: K4, p1, k2, p1, k9, p1, k2, p1, k4.
Row 8: P4, k1, p2, k11, p2, k1, p4.
Repeat rows 1–2 twice more. Work rows 13–70 from the chart provided, beginning with a knit row and working in stocking (stockinette) stitch (knit on RS, purl on WS) unless indicated otherwise. Change colours using the intarsia technique as indicated.
Row 71: K22, wrap st, turn, purl to end.
Row 72: P19, wrap st, turn, knit to end.
Row 73: K16, wrap st, turn, purl to end.
Row 74: P13, wrap st, turn, knit to end.

Row 75: K9, wrap st, turn, purl to end.
Row 76: P5, wrap st, turn, knit to end.
Row 77: Knit, getting rid of wraps as you do so.
Cast (bind) off.

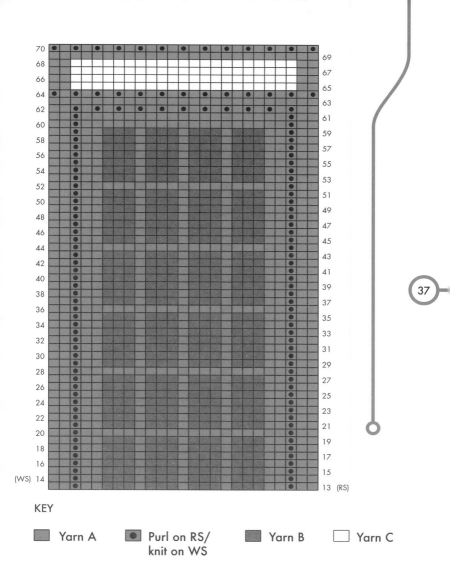

KEY

■ Yarn A ● Purl on RS/knit on WS ■ Yarn B □ Yarn C

BACK

Using A, cast on 25 sts.

Row 1 (RS): K4, p1, k15, p1, k4.

Row 2: P4, k1, p15, k1, p4.

Repeat rows 1–2 five more times.

Row 13: K4, p1, k2, p11, k2, p1, k4.

Row 14: P4, k1, p2, k1, p9, k1, p2, k1, p4.

Row 15: K4, p1, k2, p1, k9, p1, k2, p1, k4.

Row 16: P4, k1, p2, k1, p9, k1, p2, k1, p4.

Repeat rows 15–16 twenty-one more times.

Row 59: K4, p1, k2, p11, k2, p1, k4.

Row 60: P4, k1, p15, k1, p4.

Row 61: K4, p1, k15, p1, k4.

Work rows 62–70 from the chart provided, beginning with a knit row and working in stocking (stockinette) stitch (knit on RS, purl on WS) unless indicated otherwise. Change colours using the intarsia technique as indicated.

Row 71: K22, wrap st, turn, purl to end.

Row 72: P19, wrap st, turn, knit to end.

Row 73: K16, wrap st, turn, purl to end.

Row 74: P13, wrap st, turn, knit to end.

Row 75: K9, wrap st, turn, purl to end.

Row 76: P5, wrap st, turn, knit to end.

Row 77: Knit, getting rid of wraps as you do so.

Cast (bind) off.

BASE

Using B, cast on 25 sts.
Row 1 (RS): Knit.
Row 2: Purl.
Repeat last two rows until work measures 9cm (3½in) from cast-on edge.
Cast (bind) off.

ROOF

Using A, cast on 25 sts.
Row 1 (RS): Knit.
Row 2: Purl.
Repeat last two rows until work measures 9cm (3½in) from cast-on edge.
Cast (bind) off.

FINISHING

You should have three side pieces (A, B and C) and one back piece (D). Using mattress stitch and the photographs as a guide, sew the right-hand edge of A to the left-hand edge of B. Sew the right-hand edge of B to the left-hand edge of C. Sew the right-hand edge of C to the left-hand edge of D. You will now have a strip of four pieces. Sew the right-hand edge of D to the left-hand edge of A to form the box shape.

Sew the base to the bottom edge of the box. Insert the foam so that it fills the box up to the top of the white 'TELEPHONE' sign. Sew the roof to the top of the box, leaving one side open. Insert wadding (batting) and sew the final seam.

Using yarn B, embroider 'TELEPHONE' onto the white section of each of the three sides.

SEE PAGE 37 FOR CHART

THE GHERKIN

MEASUREMENTS
Height: 50cm (19¾in)
Circumference: 43cm (17in)
at widest point

YARN
Three 50g (115m/126yd) balls
of Rowan Cashsoft DK
in Blink 534 (A);
Two 100g (210m/230yd) balls
of Patons Cotton DK
in Black 2712 (B);
One 50g (140m/153yd) ball
of Rowan Siena 4ply
in Frost 653 (C)

MATERIALS
One pair each of 3.25mm
(US 3), 4mm (US 6), 4.5mm
(US 7) and 5mm (US 8)
knitting needles;
Five stitch markers;
Tapestry needle;
Foam and wadding (batting);
12cm (4¾in) diameter
circle of grey felt

TENSION (GAUGE)
This pattern is knitted using a
variety of needle sizes to obtain
the desired shape and therefore
the tension (gauge) will change
throughout. The stitch tension
(gauge) of each needle size,
using yarn double over stocking
(stockinette) stitch, is:
3.25mm (US 3) needles –
22 stitches to 10cm (4in);
4mm (US 6) needles –
20 stitches to 10cm (4in);
4.5mm (US 7) needles –
18 stitches to 10cm (4in);
5mm (US 8) needles –
16 stitches to 10cm (4in).

ABBREVIATIONS
See page 94

USE YARNS
A AND B
DOUBLE
THROUGHOUT

TOWER

The tower is made up of four wide sections using A and four narrow sections using B.

Wide Sections (make 4)

Using 3.25mm (US 3) needles and a double strand of A, cast on 13 sts.
Row 1 (RS): Knit.
Row 2: Purl.
Row 3: K2tog, k to last st, m1, k1.
Row 4: Purl.
Row 5: Knit.
Row 6: Purl.
Repeat rows 3–6 six more times.
Change to 4mm (US 6) needles.
Row 31: K2tog, k to last st, m1, k1.
Row 32: Purl.
Row 33: Knit.
Row 34: Purl.
Repeat rows 31–34 six more times.
Change to 4.5mm (US 7) needles.
Row 59: K2tog, k to last st, m1, k1.
Row 60: Purl.
Row 61: Knit.
Row 62: Purl.
Repeat rows 59–62 six more times.

Change to 5mm (US 8) needles.
Row 87: K2tog, k to last st, m1, k1.
Row 88: Purl.
Row 89: Knit.
Row 90: Purl.
Repeat rows 87–90 three more times.
Change to 4mm (US 6) needles.
Row 103: K2tog, k to last st, m1, k1.
Row 104: Purl.
Row 105: Knit.
Row 106: Purl.
Repeat rows 103–106 three more times.
Change to 3.25mm (US 3) needles.
Row 119: K2tog, k to last st, m1, k1.
Row 120: Purl.
Row 121: Knit.
Row 122: Purl.
Repeat rows 119–122 twice more.
Cast (bind) off.

Narrow Sections (make 4)

Using 3.25mm (US 3) needles and a double strand of B, cast on 7 sts.
Work as for rows 1–130 of the wide sections.
Cast (bind) off.

ROOF

Using 4.5mm (US 7) needles and a double strand of B, cast on 71 sts.

Row 1 (RS): Knit.
Row 2: Purl.
Repeat last two rows twice more.
Place markers on 8th, 22nd, 36th, 50th and 64th stitches.
Row 7: Knit, dec 1 st either side of each marked stitch. (61 sts)
Row 8: Purl.
Row 9: Knit.
Row 10: Purl.
Row 11: Knit, dec 1 st either side of each marked stitch. (51 sts)
Repeat rows 8–11 three more times. (21 sts)
Row 24: Purl.
Row 25: Knit.
Row 26: Purl.
Row 27: K2tog, k1, [k3tog, k1] to last 2 sts, k2tog. (11 sts)
Row 28: Purl.
Break off yarn, thread through stitches and pull together.

FINISHING

Lay the eight wide and narrow sections of the tower onto a flat surface, starting with a wide section on the far left and then alternating them. Call the wide section on the far left A, the narrow section next to it B, the wide section next to that C, and so on. You should have A–H.

Using mattress stitch and the photographs as a guide, sew the right-hand edge of A to the left-hand edge of B. Sew the right-hand edge of B to the left-hand edge of C. Sew the right-hand edge of C to the left-hand edge of D. Continue in this way until all eight sections are joined. You will now have a strip of eight pieces. Finally, sew the right-hand edge of H to the left-hand edge of A to form the tower shape.

Insert the foam and wadding (batting) into the tower. Use the foam to provide a firm internal structure, with wadding (batting) around it to achieve the required curved shape. Place the roof on top of the tower, insert a little more wadding (batting) into the roof and slipstitch the roof into place around the top of the tower. Sew a circle of felt to the bottom of the tower.

Using yarn C, embroider the diagonal line details onto the tower and roof using long stitches. Start by stitching along the joins of the sections and along the centre of the wide sections. When you have done this, stitch diagonals going the opposite way. The stitching on the roof should be an extension of the stitching on the tower. Finish off by sewing two parallel lines around the base of the roof.

> The Gherkin's spiral pattern is created by each floor being rotated slightly relative to the floor below.

THE KNITTY GRITTY
Here are a few top facts about the Gherkin and its surrounding area, the City of London.

The Gherkin's street address is 30 St Mary Axe.

The building was designed by Norman Foster and opened in May 2004.

It has been nicknamed the 'Gherkin' by Londoners since building work started.

The Gherkin is situated in the financial district of London, also called the City of London, or the Square Mile.

The boundaries of the Square Mile have remained almost unchanged since the Middle Ages.

BIG BEN

MEASUREMENTS
Height: 54cm (21¼in)
Width/Depth: 15cm (6in)
across clock section

YARN
Two 50g (120m/131yd) ball of
Patons Diploma Gold DK
in Natural 6143 (A);
One 50g (85m/93yd) ball of
Rowan Handknit Cotton in each
of Black 252 (B), Slate 347 (C)
and Bleached 263 (D)

MATERIALS
One pair of 4mm (US 6)
knitting needles;
Tapestry needle;
Foam and wadding (batting)

TENSION (GAUGE)
22 stitches and 30 rows to
10cm (4in) over stocking
(stockinette) stitch using
4mm (US 6) needles.

ABBREVIATIONS
See pages 94–95 for
abbreviations and information
on the intarsia technique.

NOTE
Slip stitches purlwise on
RS rows and purl them
on WS rows.

Big Ben, originally the
nickname of the bell that
chimes the hour, now
usually refers to the
whole clock tower.

ORANGES & LEMONS

Big Ben is the largest four-faced chiming clock in the world. London is famous for its bells – this traditional rhyme is said to refer to King Henry VIII and his many wives.

Oranges and lemons,
say the bells of St. Clement's.

You owe me five farthings,
say the bells of St. Martin's.

When will you pay me?
Say the bells of Old Bailey.

When I grow rich,
say the bells of Shoreditch.

When will that be?
Say the bells of Stepney.

I do not know,
says the great bell of Bow.

Here comes a candle to light you to bed, and here comes a chopper to chop off your head!

MAIN TOWER
(worked all in one piece)
Using A, cast on 114 sts.
Row 1 (RS): K24, sl1, [k27, sl1] three times, k5.
Row 2: P10, *[k1, p1] nine times, k1, p9, rep from * twice more, [k1, p1] nine times, k2. Repeat last two rows seven more times.
Row 17: K24, sl1, [k27, sl1] three times, k5.
Row 18: Knit (this creates a ridge).
Row 19: K24, sl1, [k27, sl1] three times, k5.
Row 20: P10, *[k1, p1] nine times, k1, p9, rep from * twice more, [k1, p1] nine times, k2.
Row 21: K24, sl1, [k27, sl1] three times, k5.
Row 22: Knit (this creates a ridge).
Repeat rows 1–22 three more times.
Repeat rows 1–17 once more.
Cast (bind) off.

CLOCK SECTION
(worked all in one piece)

Using A and with RS facing, pick up and knit 114 sts along cast-off (bound-off) edge of tower.

Row 1 (WS): Purl.

Row 2: K5, m1, k11, m1, k8, m1, sl1, m1, [k8, m1, k11, m1, k8, m1, sl1, m1] three times, k5. (130 sts)

Row 3: Knit (this creates a ridge).

Row 4: K27, sl1, [k31, sl1] three times, k6.

Row 5: P12, *[k1, p1] ten times, k1, p11, rep from * twice more, [k1, p1] ten times, k2.

Row 6: K27, sl1, [k31, sl1] three times, k6.

Joining in B and changing colours using the intarsia technique, continue as follows:

Row 7: P12 using A, p21 using B, [p11 using A, p21 using B] twice, p11 using A, p22 using B.

Row 8: K22 using B, [k5, sl1, k5 using A, k21 using B] three times, k5, sl1, k6 using A.

Row 9: P12 using A, p21 using B, [p11 using A, p21 using B] twice, p11 using A, p22 using B.

Repeat last two rows ten more times.

Break off B and continue in A only as follows:

Row 30: K27, sl1, [k31, sl1] three times, k6.

Row 31: P12, *[k1, p1] ten times, k1, p11, rep from * twice more, [k1, p1] ten times, k2.

Row 32: K27, sl1, [k31, sl1] three times, k6.

Row 33: Purl.

Row 34: Knit, dec 1 st either side of slipped stitches. (122 sts)

Row 35: Purl.

Repeat last two rows once more. (114 sts)

Do not cast (bind) off.

ROOF
(worked all in one piece)
Working on the stitches from the clock section, change to C and continue for the roof as follows:

Row 1 (RS): Knit.

Row 2: Knit (this creates a ridge).

Row 3: Knit, dec 1 st either side of slipped stitches. (106 sts)

Row 4: Purl, dec 1 st either side of slipped stitches. (98 sts)

Row 5: Knit.

Row 6: As row 4. (90 sts)

Row 7: As row 3. (82 sts)

Row 8: As row 4. (74 sts)

Change to A.

Rows 9: Knit.

Row 10: Knit (this creates a ridge).

Row 11: Knit.

Row 12: [K1, p1] to end.

Repeat last two rows once more.

Row 15: Knit.

Row 16: Knit (this creates a ridge).

Change to C.

Row 17: Knit.

Row 18: Knit (this creates a ridge).

Row 19: As row 3. (66 sts)

Row 20: Purl.

Row 21: Knit.

Row 22: Purl.

Row 23: As row 3. (58 sts)

Row 24: Purl.

Row 25: As row 3. (50 sts)
Row 26: As row 4. (42 sts)
Repeat rows 3–4 twice more. (10 sts)
Row 31: K1, [k3tog] three times. (4 sts)
Break off yarn, thread through stitches and pull together.

CLOCK FACES (make 4)

Using D, cast on 5 sts.
Row 1 (WS): Purl.
Row 2: K1, m1, k to last st, m1, k1. (7 sts)
Row 3: P1, m1, p to last st, m1, p1. (9 sts)
Repeat rows 2–3 once more and then row 2 again. (15 sts)
Row 7: Purl.
Row 8: As row 2. (17 sts)
Row 9: Purl.
Row 10: As row 2. (19 sts)
Row 11: Purl.
Row 12: Knit.
Row 13: Purl.
Row 14: K2tog, k to last 2 sts, k2tog. (17 sts)
Row 15: Purl.
Row 16: K2tog, k to last 2 sts, k2tog. (15 sts)
Row 17: P2tog, p to last 2 sts, p2tog. (13 sts)
Repeat last two rows twice more. (5 sts)
Cast (bind) off.

BASE

Using C, cast on 27 sts.
Row 1 (RS): Knit.
Row 2: Purl.
Repeat last two rows until work measures approx. 12cm (4¾in) or is large enough to cover the base of the tower.
Cast (bind) off.

FINISHING

Using mattress stich and the photographs as a guide, fold the tower into shape so that the slip stitches create the four corners of the building and sew from the cast-on edge all the way up to the tip of the roof.

Sew the four clock faces into position, placing them centrally within the four black squares. Using yarn B, embroider the details onto each clock face.

Insert wadding (batting) into the clock section through the opening at the base of the tower, making sure that you achieve the correct shape. Insert foam into the main section of the tower to provide a firm internal structure, then sew the base into place.

LONDON EYE

MEASUREMENTS
Circumference: 94cm (37in)

YARN
Two 50g (140m/153yd) balls of Rowan Siena 4ply in White 651 (A) and one ball in Frost 653 (B); Two 50g (85m/93yd) balls of Rowan Handknit Cotton in Slate 347 (C) and one ball in Black 252 (D)

MATERIALS
One pair each of 2.25mm (US 1) and 3.25mm (US 3) knitting needles; Two 30cm (11¾in) diameter three-spoke lampshade frames (see 'Framework', page 54); Tapestry needle; Wadding (batting); White wire coat hanger

TENSION (GAUGE)
Siena 4ply: 35 stitches and 45 rows to 10cm (4in) over stocking (stockinette) stitch using 2.25mm (US 1) needles. Handknit Cotton: 21 stitches and 32 rows to 10cm (4in) over stocking (stockinette) stitch using 3.25mm (US 3) needles.

ABBREVIATIONS
See page 94

USE YARN B DOUBLE THROUGHOUT

FRAMEWORK

Look at the photographs closely to see how the wheel has been constructed. Each lampshade frame (also known as a ring set) should consist of a small central ring and a 30cm (11¾in) diameter outer ring, with three spokes connecting the two rings rather like a bicycle wheel. The end of each spoke where it joins the outer ring should be bent at an angle so that the outer ring is slightly raised above the central ring. When the central rings of two frames are held together with the spokes aligned, the angle of the spokes will force the two outer rings slightly apart and create a framework that mirrors the double-ring construction of the London Eye.

CASINGS

For Outer Rings (make 2)
Using 2.25mm (US 1) needles and A, cast on 11 sts.
Row 1 (RS): Knit.
Row 2: Purl.
Repeat last two rows until work measures approx. 92cm (36¼in) or long enough to cover the outer ring of the lampshade frame.
Cast (bind) off.

For Spokes (make 3)
Using 2.25mm (US 1) needles and A, cast on 9 sts.
Row 1 (RS): Knit.
Row 2: Purl.
Repeat last two rows until work measures approx. 11cm (4¼in) or long enough to cover one spoke of the lampshade frame.
Cast (bind) off.

For Inner Rings (make 3)
Using 2.25mm (US 1) needles and A, cast on 9 sts.
Row 1 (RS): Knit.
Row 2: Purl.
Repeat last two rows until work measures approx. 3cm (1¼in) or long enough to cover a third of the central ring of the lampshade frame.
Cast (bind) off.

The wheel rotates so slowly that it does not actually stop when visitors get into and out of the pods.

54

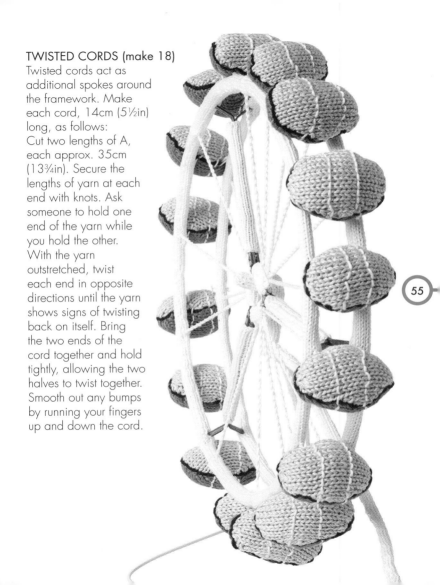

TWISTED CORDS (make 18)

Twisted cords act as additional spokes around the framework. Make each cord, 14cm (5½in) long, as follows:

Cut two lengths of A, each approx. 35cm (13¾in). Secure the lengths of yarn at each end with knots. Ask someone to hold one end of the yarn while you hold the other. With the yarn outstretched, twist each end in opposite directions until the yarn shows signs of twisting back on itself. Bring the two ends of the cord together and hold tightly, allowing the two halves to twist together. Smooth out any bumps by running your fingers up and down the cord.

ASSEMBLING
THE FRAMEWORK

Cover the outer ring of each lampshade frame with an outer ring casing. The casing will naturally roll because it is stocking (stockinette) stitch and so it will curl around the metal ring. Sew the seam using mattress stitch.

Hold the two central rings of the frames together so that the spokes align and the angle of the spokes forces the two outer rings apart. Cover each pair of aligned spokes with one of the spoke casings and sew in place to hold the two frames together. You might find this a bit easier if someone holds the frames together while you are sewing.

Cover the three sections of the centre rings (between the spokes) with the remaining casings in the same way as for the outer rings.

The framework has three sections, divided by the three main spokes. Sew one end of six twisted cords, evenly spaced, around the centre ring in each section. Sew the remaining end of the first cord to one of the outer rings of the framework, then sew the remaining end of the next cord to the other outer ring of the framework. Do this for each cord, alternating which outer ring you sew the ends to as you move around the framework, until all 18 cords have been sewn into place. Make sure that the cords are evenly spaced around both rings and that they are taut and do not sag.

NOTE FOR ASSEMBLING THE FRAMEWORK
The assembly instructions for the framework describe how to attach the casings first and then the twisted cords. However, you might find it neater to sew the cords into place as you are sewing the seams of the casings, because then you can trap the ends of the cords in the seams as you go along. This is not difficult to do but it is a little more fiddly.

PODS
Lower Sections of Pods
(make 16)
Using 3.25mm (US 3) needles and C, cast on 5 sts.
Row 1 (WS): Purl.
Row 2: [K1, m1] four times, k1. (9 sts)
Row 3: Purl.
Row 4: K1, m1, k to last st, m1, k1. (11 sts)
Row 5: Purl.
Row 6: Knit.
Row 7: Purl.
Row 8: K1, m1, k to last st, m1, k1. (13 sts)
Row 9: Purl
Row 10: K1, m1, k to last st, m1, k1. (15 sts)
Row 11: Purl.
Row 12: Knit.
Row 13: Purl.
Row 14: K2tog, k to last 2 sts, k2tog. (13 sts)
Row 15: Purl.
Row 16: K2tog, k to last 2 sts, k2tog. (11 sts)
Row 17: Purl.
Row 18: Knit.
Row 19: Purl.
Row 20: K2tog, k to last 2 sts, k2tog. (9 sts)
Row 21: Purl.

Row 22: [K2tog] twice, k1, [k2tog] twice. (5 sts)
Row 23: Purl.
Cast (bind) off.

Upper Sections of Pods
(make 16)
Using 3.25mm (US 3) needles and a double strand of B, cast on 5 sts.
Work as for lower sections of pods.

ASSEMBLING THE PODS
Each pod is made up of a dark grey lower section and a light grey upper section. When sewn together, they form an egg shape. Using mattress stitch and the photographs as a guide, join the two sections together by sewing around the side edges, leaving a small opening for inserting the wadding (batting). Once stuffed, sew the remaining seam. Do this for all 16 pods.

Using yarn D, embroider a black line around the seam of each pod. Then using yarn A, embroider two parallel lines around the centre of each pod, in the opposite direction to the black line.

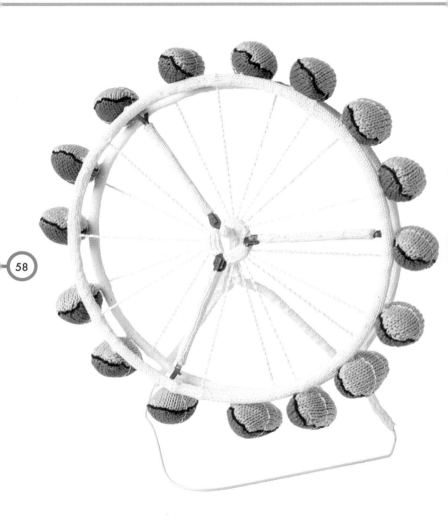

FINISHING THE WHEEL

Attach the pods to the framework, sewing each one to both of the outer rings. Place one pod at 12 o'clock, 3 o'clock, 6 o'clock and 9 o'clock positions, and then sew three pods evenly spaced in each quarter. The light grey upper section of each pod always needs to face upwards to mirror the action of the pods always staying upright as the wheel turns.

MAKING THE STAND

Turn a wire coat hanger into a stand for the wheel, taking care when bending the wire in case there are any sharp edges. With the hanger in front of you, forming a triangular shape with the hook at the top, push the two bottom corners of the triangle together, essentially folding the hanger in half. Do not fold it in half completely, but instead allow the corners to spring back slightly so that the bottom long edge of the hanger will rest flat on a surface. Straighten the hook and then re-bend it to create an upturned hook for the centre ring of the wheel to rest on – the wheel will hang on the opposite side to the 'legs' of the stand.

Casings for Legs (make 2)

Using 2.25mm (US 1) needles and A, cast on 7 sts.
Row 1 (RS): Knit.
Row 2: Purl.
Repeat last two rows until work measures approx. 22cm (8¾in) or long enough to cover hanger from base of hook to bent corner. Cast (bind) off.

Casing for Hook (make 1)

Using 2.25mm (US 1) needles and A, cast on 7 sts.
Row 1 (RS): Knit.
Row 2: Purl.
Repeat last two rows until work measures length of hook. Cast (bind) off.

ASSEMBLING THE STAND

Cover the hook with the hook casing. The casing will naturally roll because it is stocking (stockinette) stitch and so it will curl around the hook. Sew the seam using mattress stitch. Cover one leg of the stand (from base of hook casing to bent corner) with a leg casing, then sew the seam. Repeat for the other leg. Suspend the wheel on the hook.

TOWER BRIDGE

MEASUREMENTS

Height: 39cm (15½in)
Depth: 18cm (7in) at base
of main towers
Width: 80cm (31½in)
fully extended

YARN

Five 100g (210m/230yd) balls
of Patons Cotton DK in
Limestone 2716 (A);
Two 50g (115m/126yd)
balls of Rowan Cashsoft DK
in Blink 534 (B);
One 50g (125m/137yd)
ball of Rowan Pure
Wool DK in Pier 006 (C)

MATERIALS

One pair of 3.25mm (US 3)
knitting needles;
Two 3.75mm (US 5)
double-pointed needles;
Tapestry needle and pins;
Foam and wadding (batting);
Two 7.5 x 15cm (3 x 6in) and
one 7.5 x 24cm (3 x 9½in)
pieces of grey felt

TENSION (GAUGE)

25 stitches and 34 rows to
10cm (4in) over stocking
(stockinette) stitch using
3.25mm (US 3) needles.

ABBREVIATIONS

See pages 94–95 for
abbreviations and
information on charts
and the intarsia technique.

NOTE

Slip stitches purlwise

SEE PAGES 64–65 FOR CHARTS

MAIN TOWERS (make 2)
Fronts (make 2 for each tower)
Using 3.25 (US 3) needles,
cast on 23 sts as follows:
9 sts using A, 5 sts using B,
9 sts using A.
Work all 79 rows of the main
tower front chart provided,
beginning with a knit row and
working in stocking (stockinette)
stitch (knit on RS, purl on WS)
unless indicated otherwise.
Change colours using the intarsia
technique as indicated. When
completed, cast (bind) off.

Sides (make 2 for each tower)
Using 3.25 (US 3) needles, cast
on 29 sts as follows:
7 sts using A, 15 sts using B,
7 sts using A.
Work all 79 rows of the main
tower side chart provided,
beginning with a knit row and
working in stocking (stockinette)
stitch (knit on RS, purl on WS)
unless indicated otherwise.
Change colours using the intarsia
technique as indicated. When
completed, cast (bind) off.

ROOF OF MAIN TOWERS
Turrets (make 4 for each tower)
Using 3.25 (US 3) needles
and A, cast on 21 sts.
Row 1 (RS): K5, [sl1, k4] twice,
sl1, k5.
Row 2: Purl.
Repeat last two rows three
more times.
Change to B.
Row 9: K5, [sl1, k4] twice,
sl1, k5.
Row 10: Knit (this creates
a ridge).
Change to A.
Row 11: K5, [sl1, k4] twice,
sl1, k5.
Row 12: Purl.
Repeat last two rows once more.
Row 15: K2, [k2tog, k1, sl1, k1]
three times, k2tog, k2. (17 sts)
Row 16: Purl.
Row 17: K4, [sl1, k3] twice,
sl1, k4.
Row 18: Purl.
Repeat last two rows once more.
Row 21: K1, [k3tog, sl1] three
times, k3tog, k1. (9 sts)
Row 22: Purl.
Row 23: K2tog, sl1, k3tog, sl1,
k2tog. (5 sts)
Row 24: P1, p3tog, p1. (3 sts)
Row 25: K3tog.
Fasten off.

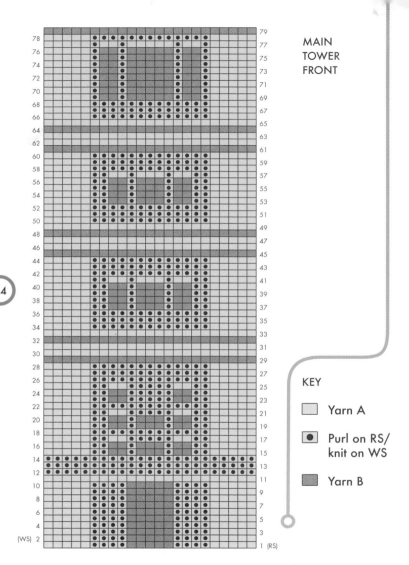

MAIN
TOWER
FRONT

64

KEY

Yarn A

● Purl on RS/
knit on WS

Yarn B

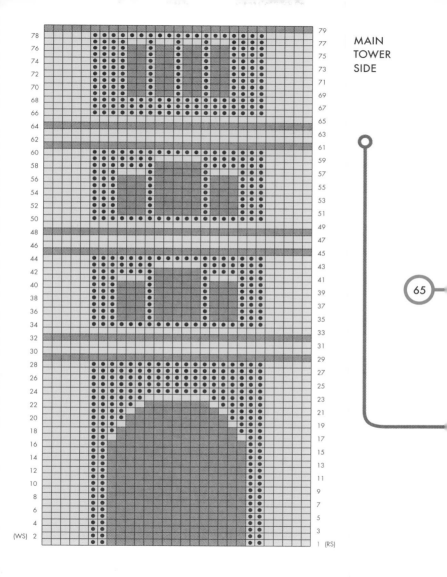

65

Flat Roof
(make 1 for each tower)
Using 3.25 (US 3) needles
and A, cast on 23 sts.
Row 1 (RS): Knit.
Row 2: Purl.
Repeat last two rows until work
measures 11cm (4¼in).
Cast (bind) off.

Wider Panels of Pitched Roof
(make 2 for each tower)
Using 3.25 (US 3) needles
and B, cast on 19 sts.
Row 1 (RS): Knit.
Row 2: Purl.
Repeat last two rows twice more.
Row 7: K2tog, k to last 2 sts,
k2tog. (17 sts)
Row 8: Purl.
Row 9: Knit.
Row 10: Purl.
Repeat last two rows twice more.
Row 15: K2tog, k to last 2 sts,
k2tog. (15 sts)
Row 16: Purl.
Row 17: Knit.
Row 18: Purl.
Row 19: K2tog, k to last 2 sts,
k2tog. (13 sts)
Repeat rows 16–19 twice
more. (9 sts)
Row 28: Purl.
Row 29: K2tog, k to last 2 sts,
k2tog. (7 sts)

Row 30: Purl.
Row 31: K2tog, k to last 2 sts,
k2tog. (5 sts)
Row 32: Purl.
Row 33: K1, k3tog, k1. (3 sts)
Row 34: Purl.
Row 35: K3tog.
Fasten off.

Narrow Panels of Pitched Roof
(make 2 for each tower)
Using 3.25 (US 3) needles
and B, cast on 15 sts.
Row 1 (RS): Knit.
Row 2: Purl.
Repeat last two rows twice more.
Row 7: K2tog, k to last 2 sts,
k2tog. (13 sts)
Row 8: Purl.
Row 9: Knit.
Row 10: Purl.
Repeat last two rows twice more.
Row 15: K2tog, k to last 2 sts,
k2tog. (11 sts)
Row 16: Purl.
Row 17: Knit.
Row 18: Purl.
Row 19: K2tog, k to last 2 sts,
k2tog. (9 sts)
Repeat rows 16–19 twice
more. (5 sts)
Row 28: Purl.
Row 29: Knit.
Row 30: Purl.
Repeat last two rows once more.

Row 33: K1, k3tog, k1. (3 sts)
Row 34: Purl.
Row 35: K3tog.
Fasten off.

BASE OF MAIN TOWERS
Flat Sections
(make 2 for each tower)
Using 3.25 (US 3) needles
and A, cast on 13 sts.
Row 1 (RS): Knit.
Row 2: Purl.
Row 3: K1, m1, k to last st,
m1, k1. (15 sts)
Repeat last two rows six more
times (27 sts)
Row 16: Purl.
Row 17: Knit.
Row 18: Purl.
Repeat last two rows until work
measures 14cm (5½in).

Next row: K2tog, k to last 2 sts,
k2tog. (25 sts)
Next row: Purl.
Next row: K2tog, k to last 2 sts,
k2tog. (23 sts)
Repeat last two rows five more
times. (13 sts)
Next row: Purl.
Cast (bind) off.

Side Section
(make 1 for each tower)
Using 3.25 (US 3) needles
and A, cast on 21 sts.
Row 1 (RS): Knit.
Row 2: Purl.
Repeat last two rows until
work measures 50cm (19¾in).
Cast (bind) off.

> Completed in 1894, the
> central road section of
> Tower Bridge can be
> raised to allow river
> traffic to pass.

SMALL TOWERS (make 2)
Fronts (make 2 for each tower)
Using 3.25 (US 3) needles
and A, cast on 13 sts.
Row 1 (RS): P4, k5, p4.
Row 2: K4, p5, k4.
Repeat last two rows thirteen
more times.
Change to B.
Row 29: Knit.
Change to A.
Row 30: Purl.
Row 31: P4, k5, p4.
Row 32: K4, p5, k4.
Repeat last rows once more.
Cast (bind) off.

Sides (make 2 for each tower)
Using 3.25 (US 3) needles,
cast on 29 sts as follows:
7 sts using A, 15 sts using B,
7 sts using A.
Work all 34 rows of the small
tower side chart provided,
working the chart in the usual
way. When completed, cast
(bind) off.

ROOF OF SMALL TOWER
Flat Roof (make 1 for
each tower)
Using 3.25 (US 3) needles
and A, cast on 29 sts.
Row 1 (RS): Knit.
Row 2: Purl.

Repeat last two rows until work
measures 5cm (2in).
Cast (bind) off.

Wider Panels of Pitched Roof
(make 2 for each tower)
Using 3.25 (US 3) needles
and B, cast on 25 sts.
Row 1 (RS): Knit.
Row 2: Purl.
Row 3: K2tog, k to last 2 sts,
k2tog. (23 sts)
Row 4: Purl.
Row 5: Knit.
Row 6: Purl.
Row 7: K2tog, k to last 2 sts,
k2tog. (21 sts)
Repeat rows 4–7 once more and
then rows 4–6 again. (19 sts)
Row 15: Purl (this creates
a ridge).
Row 16: Purl.
Row 17: Knit.
Row 18: Purl.
Row 19: K1, m1, k to last st,
m1, k1. (21 sts)
Repeat rows 16–19 twice
more. (25 sts)
Row 28: Purl.
Row 29: Knit.
Cast (bind) off purlwise.

SMALL TOWER SIDE

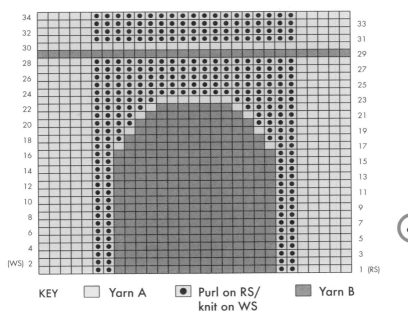

KEY ☐ Yarn A   ● Purl on RS/ knit on WS   ▨ Yarn B

Narrow Panels of Pitched Roof
(make 2 for each tower)
Using 3.25 (US 3) needles
and B, cast on 11 sts.
Row 1 (RS): Knit.
Row 2: Purl.
Repeat last two rows once more.
Row 5: K2tog, k to last 2 sts,
k2tog. (9 sts)

Row 6: Purl.
Row 7: K2tog, k to last 2 sts,
k2tog. (7 sts)
Repeat last two rows twice
more. (3 sts)
Row 12: Purl.
Row 13: K3tog.
Fasten off.

BASE OF SMALL TOWERS
Flat Sections
(make 1 for each tower)
Using 3.25 (US 3) needles
and A, cast on 29 sts.
Row 1 (RS): Knit.
Row 2: Purl.
Repeat last two rows until work
measures 5cm (2in).
Cast (bind) off.

Side Section
(make 1 for each tower)
Using 3.25 (US 3) needles
and A, cast on 21 sts.
Row 1 (RS): Knit.
Row 2: Purl.
Repeat last two rows until work
measures 30cm (11¾in).
Cast (bind) off.

ROADS
Short Sections (make 2)
Using 3.25 (US 3) needles
and B, cast on 19 sts.
Row 1 (RS): Knit.
Row 2: Purl.
Repeat last two rows until work
measures 15cm (6in).
Cast (bind) off.

Long Section (make 1)
Using 3.25 (US 3) needles
and B, cast on 19 sts.
Row 1 (RS): Knit.

Row 2: Purl.
Repeat last two rows until work
measures 24cm (9½in).
Cast (bind) off.

RAILINGS
**(make 4 short railings
and 4 long railings)**
These are used to edge the roads
and join the tops of the two main
towers. Each railing is made from
an i-cord as follows:
Using 3.75mm (US 5) double-
pointed needles and C, cast
on 5 sts.
Row 1 (RS): Knit.
You would now usually turn the
needles to work the next row,
but to make an i-cord DO NOT
TURN. Instead, slide the stitches
to the other end of the double-

pointed needle, ready to be knitted again. The yarn will now be at the left edge of the knitting, and so to knit the next row you must pull the yarn tightly across the back of the work and then knit one more row. Continue in this way, never turning and always sliding the work to the other end of the double-pointed needle. The right side of the work will always be facing you. Repeat row 1 until cord is the required length.

Make four short i-cord railings, each 15cm (6in) long, and four long i-cord railings, each 24cm (9½in) long.

Break off yarn, thread through stitches and pull together.

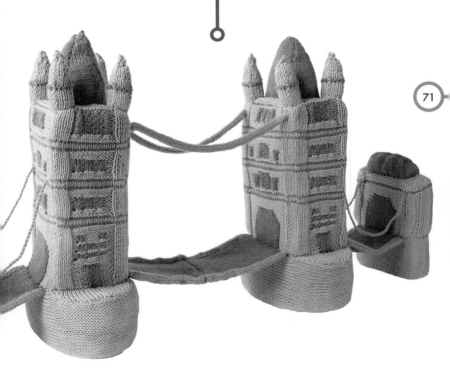

CABLES (make 4)

These are used to connect the tops of the small towers with the main towers. Make four twisted cords, each 28cm (11in) long, as follows:

Cut two lengths of C, each approx. 70cm (27½in). Secure the lengths of yarn at each end with knots. Ask someone to hold one end of the yarn while you hold the other. With the yarn outstretched, twist each end in opposite directions until the yarn shows signs of twisting back on itself. Bring the two ends of the cord together and hold tightly, allowing the two halves to twist together. Smooth out any bumps by running your fingers up and down the cord.

ASSEMBLING THE TOWERS
Main Towers

Each main tower has two front sections and two side sections. Lay these four sections next to each other as follows: side section (A), front section (B), side section (C), front section (D). Using mattress stitch and the photographs as a guide, sew the right-hand edge of A to the left-hand edge of B. Sew the right-hand edge of B to the left-hand edge of C. Sew the right-hand edge of C to the left-hand edge of D. You will now have a strip of four pieces. Finally, sew the right-hand edge of D to the left-hand edge of A to form the tower. Do this for both main towers.

Sew the flat roof to the top of the tower. Insert wadding (batting) into the turrets and sew one turret to each corner of the flat roof. Sew the four sections of the pitched roof together (the two wider panels are joined by sewing the smaller panels to each side). Insert wadding (batting) into the pitched roof, then sew the pitched roof into place at the centre of the flat roof (inside the turrets), with the wider panels in line with the sides of the tower. Do this for both main towers.

The base for each main tower has two flat sections (A and B) and one side section (C). Sew one of the side edges of C to the side edges of A, starting at the centre of A's cast-on edge and continuing all the way around until you get back to the starting point. The cast-on and cast-off (bound-off) edges of C will now meet – slipstitch these together. Insert foam and finish by sewing B to the remaining edge of C in the same way that you attached A. Do this for both main towers.

Small Towers

Each small tower has two front sections and two side sections. Lay these four sections next to each other as follows: side section (A), front section (B), side section (C), front section (D). Using mattress stitch, sew the right-hand edge of A to the left-hand edge of B. Sew the right-hand edge of B to the left-hand edge of C. Sew the right-hand edge of C to the left-hand edge of D. You will now have a strip of four pieces. Finally, sew the right-hand edge of D to the left-hand edge of A to form the tower. Do this for both small towers.

Sew the flat roof to the top of the tower. Sew the four sections of the pitched roof together (the two wider panels are joined by sewing the smaller panels to each side). Insert wadding (batting) and then sew into place at the centre of the flat roof, with the wider panels in line with the sides of the tower.

The base for each small tower has one flat section (A) and one side section (B). Sew one of the side edges of B to the cast-on edges of the assembled tower, starting at the centre of the cast-on edge of one of the tower's side sections and continuing all the way around until you get back to the starting point. The cast-on and cast-off (bound-off) edges of B will now meet – slipstitch these together. Insert foam and finish by sewing A to the remaining edge of B in the same way that you attached it to the cast-on edge of the tower. Do this for both small towers.

ASSEMBLING THE BRIDGE

You should have two short road sections and one long road section. Cut the felt to the size of each section and pin to the wrong side of the knitted pieces. Slipstitch into place. Sew one of the short railings along each edge of the short road sections. Sew one of the long railings along each edge of the long road section.

Using the photographs as a guide, set out the four towers, starting with a small tower, then the two main towers and then the other small tower.

Sew the cast-on edge of the first small road section to the side of the first small tower where the base meets the tower (at base of grey arch). Then join the cast-off (bound-off) edge of the road to the side of the first main tower,

again at the base of the grey arch. One of the main towers will now be joined to one of the small towers. Do this for the other main and small tower. You will now need to join the two main towers using the long section of road.

Sew the cast-on edge of the long road section to the side edge of one of the main towers (again at base of grey arch) and then sew the cast-off (bound-off) edge to the same place on the other main tower.

Finally, attach the four twisted cord cables, one pair between each small and main tower. Then take the two remaining long railings and sew into place between the roofs of the main towers, parallel with the long road section.

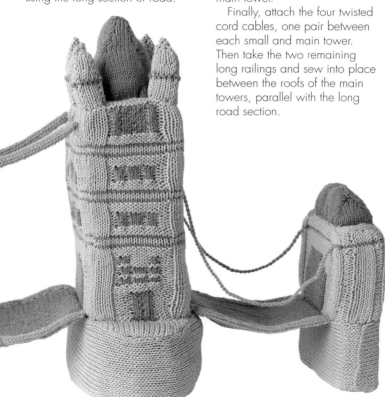

CHANGING THE GUARD

MEASUREMENTS
Guard height: 26cm (10¼in)
Box height: 26cm (10¼in)
Box width: 13cm (5¼in)

YARN
Two 50g (115m/126yd) balls of
Rowan Cotton Glacé
in Black 727 (A), one ball
in Poppy 741 (B) and one ball
in Oyster 730 (C);
One 25g (210m/229yd) ball
of Rowan Kidsilk Haze
in Wicked 599 (D)

TENSION (GAUGE)
30 stitches and 38 rows to
10cm (4in) over stocking
(stockinette) stitch using
2.75mm (US 2) needles.

MATERIALS
One pair each of 2.75mm
(US 2) and 3mm (US 2/3)
knitting needles;
Two 3.25mm (US 3)
double-pointed needles;
Tapestry needle;
Foam and wadding (batting);
Stitch marker and stitch holder;
9cm (3½in) length of craft wire;
16cm (6¼in) length of 5mm
(¼in) wide white ribbon;
Sewing needle and thread;
Seven small gold beads;
7cm (2¾in) length of
small gold chain;
26 x 13cm (10¼ x 5¼in)
piece of grey felt

ABBREVIATIONS
See page 94

NOTE
Slip stitches purlwise

DOLL
Body (make 2)
Using 2.75mm (US 2) needles and C, cast on 7 sts.

Row 1 (WS): Purl.
Row 2: [K1, m1, k2, m1] twice, k1. (11 sts)
Row 3: Purl.
Row 4: K1, m1, k9, m1, k1. (13 sts)
Row 5: Purl.
Row 6: K1, m1, k11, m1, k1. (15 sts)
Row 7: Purl.
Row 8: Knit.
Row 9: Purl.
Repeat last two rows until work measures 6.5cm (2½in) from cast-on edge, ending with a WS row.
Next row (RS): K2tog, k to last 2 sts, k2tog. (13 sts)
Next row: Purl.
Next row: K2tog, k to last 2 sts, k2tog. (11 sts)
Next row: P2tog, p to last 2 sts, p2tog. (9 sts)
Next row: [K3tog] three times. (3 sts)
Cast (bind) off.

Head (make 2)
Using 2.75mm (US 2) needles and C, cast on 3 sts.

Row 1 (WS): Purl.
Row 2: [K1, m1] twice, k1. (5 sts)
Row 3: Purl.
Row 4: [K1, m1] four times, k1. (9 sts)
Row 5: Purl.
Row 6: K1, m1, k to last st, m1, k1. (11 sts)
Row 7: Purl.
Row 8: Knit.
Row 9: Purl.
Repeat last two rows twice more.
Row 14: K2tog, k to last 2 sts, k2tog. (9 sts)
Row 15: Purl.
Row 16: K2tog, k to last 2 sts, k2tog. (7 sts)
Row 17: Purl.
Row 18: K2tog, k to last 2 sts, k2tog. (5 sts)
Cast (bind) off.

Arms (make 2)

Using 2.75mm (US 2) needles and C, cast on 3 sts.

Row 1 (WS): Purl.
Row 2: [K1, m1] twice, k1. (5 sts)
Row 3: Purl.
Row 4: K1, m1, k to last st, m1, k1. (7 sts)
Row 5: Purl.
Row 6: Knit.
Row 7: Purl.

Repeat last two rows until work measures 7cm (2¾in) from cast-on edge, ending with a WS row. Cast (bind) off, at the same time knitting 2 sts together at each end.

Legs (make 2)

Using 2.75mm (US 2) needles and C, cast on 3 sts.

Row 1 (WS): Purl.
Row 2: [K1, m1] twice, k1. (5 sts)
Row 3: Purl.
Row 4: [K1, m1] four times, k1. (9 sts)
Row 5: Purl.
Row 6: K1, m1, k7, m1, k1. (11 sts)
Row 7: Purl.
Row 8: Knit.
Row 9: Purl.

Repeat last two rows until work measures 9cm (3½in) from cast-on edge, ending with a WS row. Cast (bind) off, working the cast-off (bind-off) row as follows: [K2tog] twice, k3, [k2tog] twice.

FINISHING THE DOLL

The body of the doll has been worked in two pieces. Using mattress stitch, sew the pieces together, leaving a small opening for stuffing. Insert some wadding (batting), then sew the final seam. Sew the two pieces of the head together in the same way.

Each arm has been worked in one piece. Fold each arm in half lengthways and sew the two side edges together to form a seam, leaving about a third of the seam open for stuffing. Insert some wadding (batting), then sew the final seam. Sew each leg in the same way as the arms.

Attach the arms, legs and head to the body.

JACKET
Back
Using 2.75mm (US 2) needles
and B, cast on 19 sts.
Row 1 (RS): Knit.
Row 2: Purl.
Row 3: Purl (this creates a ridge
for turning the hem back).
Row 4: Purl.
Row 5: Knit.
Row 6: Purl.
Repeat last two rows fifteen
more times.
Cast (bind) off.

Right Front
Using 2.75mm (US 2) needles
and B, cast on 10 sts.
Row 1 (RS): Knit.
Row 2: Purl.
Row 3: Purl (this creates a ridge
for turning the hem back).
Row 4: Purl.
Row 5: Knit.
Row 6: Purl.
Repeat last two rows thirteen
more times.
Row 33: Cast (bind) off 2 sts,
k to end. (8 sts)
Row 34: Purl.
Row 35: K2tog, k to end. (7 sts)
Row 36: Purl.
Cast (bind) off.

Left Front

Using 2.75mm (US 2) needles and B, cast on 10 sts.

Row 1 (RS): Knit.
Row 2: Purl.
Row 3: Purl (this creates a ridge for turning the hem back).
Row 4: Purl.
Row 5: Knit.
Row 6: Purl.
Repeat last two rows twelve more times.
Row 31: Knit.
Row 32: Cast (bind) off 2 sts, p to end. (8 sts)
Row 33: Knit.
Row 34: P2tog, p to end. (7 sts)
Row 35: Knit.
Row 36: Purl
Cast (bind) off.

Sleeves (make 2)

Using 2.75mm (US 2) needles and A, cast on 15 sts.
Row 1 (RS): Knit.
Row 2: Knit (this creates a ridge). Change to B.
Row 3: Knit.
Row 4: Purl.
Repeat last two rows eleven more times.
Cast (bind) off.

FINISHING THE JACKET

Using mattress stitch and the photographs as a guide, join the right front of the jacket to the back by sewing the cast-off (bound-off) edge of the front to the corresponding cast-off (bound-off) stitches of the back. Do the same for the left front. You will have a gap in the middle for the neck.

Fold each sleeve in half lengthways and mark the centre of the cast-off (bound-off) edge with a marker. Align this marker with the shoulder seam on the jacket and tack (baste) the sleeve in place. Sew the sleeves to the jacket. Sew the side and sleeve seams of the jacket by working up the side and then along the sleeve. Do this for both sides.

ADDING THE COLLAR

Using 2.75mm (US 2) needles and A and with RS facing, pick up and knit 6 sts up right neck, 7 sts across back neck and 6 sts down left neck (19 sts in total) and work as follows:
Row 1 (WS): Purl.
Row 2: Knit.
Cast (bind) off knitwise.

TROUSERS
Front Section – Left Leg
Using 2.75mm (US 2) needles and A, cast on 9 sts.
Row 1 (RS): Knit.
Row 2: Purl.
Repeat last two rows until work measures 8cm (3¼in) from cast-on edge.
Leave stitches on a holder.

Front Section – Right Leg
Work as for left leg but leave stitches on needle.

Front Section – Joining the Legs
With RS facing, knit across 8 sts of left leg, knit ninth stitch together with first stitch of right leg and knit remaining 8 sts of right leg. (17 sts)
Next row: Purl.
Next row: Knit.
Next row: Purl.
Repeat last two rows once more.
Next row: K2tog, k to last 2 sts, k2tog. (15 sts)
Next row: Purl.
Next row: Knit.
Next row: Purl.
Cast (bind) off.

Back Section
Work as for front section.

FINISHING THE TROUSERS
Using mattress stitch, join the front and back sections of the trousers by sewing the side seams and the inside leg seams.

BOOTS (make 2)
Using 2.75mm (US 2) needles and A, cast on 13 sts.
Row 1 (RS): Knit.
Row 2: Purl.
Row 3: K6, m1, k1, m1, k6. (15 sts)
Row 4: Purl.
Row 5: K7, m1, k1, m1, k7. (17 sts)
Row 6: P8, m1, p1, m1, p8. (19 sts)
Row 7: K9, m1, k1, m1, k9. (21 sts)
Row 8: P10, m1, p1, m1, p10. (23 sts)
Row 9: K11, m1, k1, m1, k11. (25 sts)
Row 10: P12, m1, p1, m1, p12. (27 sts)
Row 11: K13, m1, k1, m1, k13. (29 sts)
Row 12: P12, p2tog, p1, p2tog, p to end. (27 sts)
Row 13: K9, [k2tog] twice, k1, [k2tog] twice, k to end. (23 sts)
Row 14: P9, p2tog, p1, p2tog, p to end. (21 sts)
Cast (bind) off.

FINISHING THE BOOTS

Fold each boot in half and join the side seams by sewing along the underneath of the sole and up the back. Insert wadding (batting), leaving a small gap for the base of the leg to slot into.

BUSBY HAT

Using 3mm (US 2/3) needles, one strand of A and two strands of D, cast on 15 sts.
Row 1 (RS): Purl.
Row 2: Knit.
Row 3: P1, m1, p to last st, m1, p1. (17 sts)
Row 4: Knit.
Repeat last two rows once more. (19 sts)
Row 7: Purl.
Row 8: Knit.
Repeat last two rows once more.
Row 11: P2tog, p to last 2 sts, p2tog. (17 sts)
Row 12: Knit.
Repeat last two rows once more. (15 sts)
Row 15: K2tog, k to last 2 sts, k2tog. (13 sts)
Row 16: [P3tog] twice, p1, [p3tog] twice. (5 sts)
Break off yarns, thread through stitches and pull together.

FINISHING THE BUSBY HAT

The hat has been knitted in one piece. Fold the hat in half so that the side edges meet at the back to form a seam. Sew the seam using mattress stitch.

GUN

Make an i-cord as follows:
Using 3.25mm (US 3) double-pointed needles and A, cast on 3 sts.
Row 1 (RS): Knit.
You would now usually turn the needles to work the next row, but to make an i-cord DO NOT TURN. Instead, slide the stitches to the other end of the double-pointed needle, ready to be knitted again. The yarn will now be at the left edge of the knitting, and so to knit the next row you must pull the yarn tightly across the back of the work and then knit one more row. Continue in this way, never turning and always sliding the work to the other end of the double-pointed needle. The right side of the work will always be facing you. Repeat row 1 until cord measures 9cm (3½in).
Insert the craft wire into the cord, then break off yarn, thread through stitches and pull together.

DRESSING THE GUARD

Put the trousers onto the doll and use a few slipstitches to secure the waistband to the body of the doll. Put the jacket on, making sure that the fronts overlap very slightly, and slipstitch the right to the left front so that the jacket stays closed – right on top of left.

Using the photographs as a guide, wrap the white ribbon around the waist of the jacket to form a belt and slipstitch into place with a needle and thread. Sew two small gold beads to the centre front of the belt to form a buckle. Sew the remaining five gold beads to the opening of the right front jacket, starting with one at the collar and the remaining four evenly spaced between the collar and the belt.

Put the boots on by inserting the base of each leg into each boot. Use a few slipstitches to secure the boots to the legs.

Insert some wadding (batting) into the hat, making sure that you leave a gap at the base for the head to fit into. The cast-on edge of the hat should be worn halfway down the head. Attach the gold chain inside each side of the hat so that the chain hangs at chin height. Finally, sew the gun into place between the cuff of the jacket sleeve and the shoulder.

GUARD BOX

Back

Using 2.75mm (US 2) needles and A, cast on 37 sts.
Row 1 (RS): Knit.
Row 2: Purl.
Repeat last two rows four more times.
Row 11: K2tog, k to last 2 sts, k2tog. (35 sts)
Row 12: Purl.
Row 13: Knit.
Row 14: Purl.
Repeat last two rows four more times.
Row 23: K2tog, k to last 2 sts, k2tog. (33 sts)
Repeat rows 12–23 five more times. (23 sts)
Row 84: Purl.
Row 85: Knit.
Row 86: Knit (this creates a ridge).
Row 87: Knit.
Row 88: Purl.
Row 89: K2tog, k to last 2 sts, k2tog. (21 sts)
Row 90: P2tog, p to last 2 sts, p2tog. (19 sts)
Repeat last two rows four more times. (3 sts)
Row 99: K3tog.
Fasten off.

Front – Right Side of Arch

Using 2.75mm (US 2) needles and A, cast on 5 sts.
Row 1 (RS): Knit.
Row 2: Purl.
Repeat last two rows four more times.
Row 11: K1, m1, k to last 2 sts, k2tog.
Row 12: Purl.
Row 13: Knit.
Row 14: Purl.
Repeat last two rows four more times.
Row 23: K1, m1, k to last 2 sts, k2tog.
Repeat rows 12–23 three more times.
Row 60: Purl.
Row 61: Knit.
Row 62: Purl.
Repeat last two rows four more times.
Row 71: K1, m1, k to end. (6 sts)
Row 72: Purl.
Row 73: Knit.
Row 74: Purl.
Row 75: K1, m1, k to end. (7 sts)
Repeat last two rows four more times. (11 sts)
Row 84: Purl.
Do not cast (bind) off. Leave stitches on a holder.

Front – Left Side of Arch

Using 2.75mm (US 2) needles and A, cast on 5 sts.
Row 1 (RS): Knit.
Row 2: Purl.
Repeat last two rows four more times.
Row 11: K2tog, k to last st, m1, k1.
Row 12: Purl.
Row 13: Knit.
Row 14: Purl.
Repeat last two rows four more times.
Row 23: K2tog, k to last st, m1, k1.
Repeat rows 12–23 three more times.
Row 60: Purl.
Row 61: Knit.
Row 62: Purl.
Repeat last two rows four more times.
Row 71: K to last st, m1, k1. (6 sts)
Row 72: Purl.
Row 73: Knit.
Row 74: Purl.
Row 75: K to last st, m1, k1. (7 sts)
Repeat last two rows four more times. (11 sts)
Row 84: Purl.
Do not cast (bind) off. Leave stitches on a holder.

Front – Joining the Arch

Join the two sections to form an arch as follows:
Row 85 (RS): Knit across all 11 sts of left side and then all 11 sts of right side. (22 sts)
Row 86: Purl, inc 1 st in middle of row. (23 sts)
Row 87: Knit.
Row 88: Purl.
Row 89: Knit.
Row 90: Knit (this creates a ridge).
Row 91: Knit.
Row 92: Purl.
Row 93: K2tog, k to last 2 sts, k2tog. (21 sts)
Row 94: P2tog, p to last 2 sts, p2tog. (19 sts)
Repeat last two rows four more times.
Row 103: K3tog.
Fasten off.

Arch Edging

Using 3mm (US 2/3) needles and A and with RS facing, pick up and knit 118 sts around edge of the arch, starting at the bottom of the right side and working around to the bottom of the left side.
Row 1 (WS): Knit.
Cast (bind) off.

Sides (make 2)
Using 2.75mm (US 2) needles
and A, cast on 17 sts.
Row 1 (RS): Knit.
Row 2: Purl.
Repeat last two rows until work
measures 23cm (9in) from
cast-on edge.
Cast (bind) off.

Base
Using 2.75mm (US 2) needles
and A, cast on 37 sts.
Row 1 (RS): Knit.
Row 2: Purl.
Repeat last two rows until work
measures 6.5cm (2½in) from
cast-on edge.
Cast (bind) off.

Roof
Using 2.75mm (US 2) needles
and A, cast on 27 sts.
Row 1 (RS): K2, sl1, k21,
sl1, k2.
Row 2: Purl.
Repeat last two rows until
work measures 7cm (2¾in)
from cast-on edge, ending
with a WS row.
Next row (RS): Purl
(this creates a ridge).
Next row: Purl.
Next row: Knit.

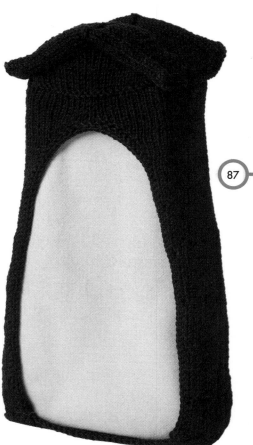

KNIT LONDON? QUIZ LONDON!

**Can you answer these questions about London?
If you get stuck, the answers are on p96.**

1. It is one of London's most famous ceremonies,
but can you list the four different sites where
Changing the Guard takes place?

2. Can you guess how many listed buildings there
are in London?

3. Can you list London's four UNESCO world
heritage sites?

4. The oldest public museum in the world was
founded in 1753 and is situated in London –
can you name it?

The ceremonial changeover
of the Queen's Guard at
Buckingham Palace attracts
thousands of visitors.

Next row: Purl.
Repeat last two rows until work measures 7cm (2¾in) from last ridge, ending with a WS row.
Next row (RS): Purl (this creates a ridge).
Next row: Purl.
Next row: Knit.
Next row: Purl.
Repeat last two rows until work measures 7cm (2¾in) from last ridge, ending with a WS row.
Next row (RS): Purl (this creates a ridge).
Next row: Purl.
Next row: Knit.
Next row: Purl.
Repeat last two rows until work measures 7cm (2¾in) from last ridge.
Cast (bind) off.

FINISHING THE ROOF

You will have a long strip that is divided into four sections by three ridges. With WS facing, fold the two outer sections (along the ridges) into the middle so that the cast-on and cast-off (bound-off) edges meet in the middle. Slipstitch them into place.

FINISHING THE GUARD BOX

With RS facing, join the sides of the box to the back – the top of each side will be level with the garter stitch ridge on the back. Join the front (arch) to the sides; again, the sides will be level with the garter stitch ridge on the front. Sew the base to the underneath of the box, making sure that you sew the cast-on edges of the arch to the base, too.

Cut the foam to the shape of the box (use the knitting as a template – the foam should be level with the garter stitch ridge on the back and front) and then insert into the box. On top of the foam, insert some wadding (batting) as this will help to keep the pitch of the roof. Attach the roof by slipstitching the edges of the triangular section of the front and back to the underside of the roof, making sure that the roof overhangs by approx. 1cm (⅜in).

The box is now constructed but you will be able to see the foam through the front arch. Cover the foam with a piece of grey felt, tucking the felt around the foam. Slipstitch the felt into place to stop it from moving around.

UNION JACK

MEASUREMENTS
Height: 16cm (6¼in)
Width: 21cm (8¼in)

YARN
One 50g (125m/137yd) ball
of Rowan Pure Wool DK
in Indigo 010 (A);
One 50g (115m/126yd)
ball of Rowan Cashsoft DK
in Poppy 512 (B);
One 50g (115m/126yd) ball of
Rowan Cashsoft Baby DK
in Snowman 800 (C)

MATERIALS
One pair of 4mm (US 6)
knitting needles;
Pins, sewing needle and
navy thread;
16 x 21cm (6¼ x 8¼in)
piece of navy felt;
Flag pole (a knitting
needle is ideal)

TENSION (GAUGE)
22 stitches and 30 rows to
10cm (4in) over stocking
(stockinette) stitch using
4mm (US 6) needles.

ABBREVIATIONS
See pages 94–95 for
abbreviations and
information on charts
and the intarsia technique.

FLAG

Cast on 47 sts as follows:
1 st using C, 2 sts using B,
1 st using C, 16 sts using A,
1 st using C, 5 sts using B,
1 st using C, 16 sts using A,
4 sts using C.
Beginning with a knit row, work in stocking (stockinette) stitch (knit on RS, purl on WS) from the chart provided, changing colours using the intarsia technique as indicated. When all 46 rows of the chart have been completed, cast (bind) off using colours as set.

FINISHING

Pin the felt to the wrong side of the flag, trimming the felt to fit the knitted piece if necessary. Slipstitch the felt into place, leaving a small gap at the top left and bottom left for the flag pole. Insert the flag pole, then add a few more stitches to hold the pole in place if required.

The current design of the flag dates from the union of Great Britain and Ireland in 1801.

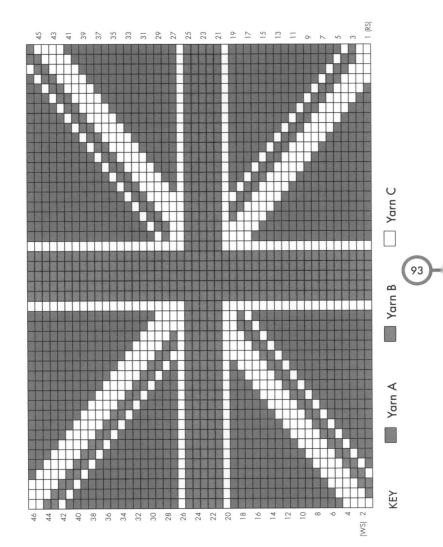

KEY

Yarn A

Yarn B

Yarn C

TECHNIQUES

All of the abbreviations and special techniques
used in the patterns are explained here.

ABBREVIATIONS

approx: approximately

cm: centimetre(s)

dec: decreas(e)(ing): you can decrease one stitch by working k2tog or p2tog

g: gram(s)

in: inch(es)

inc: increas(e)(ing): you can increase one stitch using m1

k: knit

k2(3)tog: knit two (three) stitches together

m1: make one stitch: put the tip of the left needle from front to back under the horizontal strand of yarn that stretches between the stitch just worked and the next stitch; pick up this strand with the left needle and knit or purl through the back of it to create an extra stitch on the right needle, then slip the strand off the left needle

mm: millimetre(s)

p: purl

p2(3)tog: purl two (three) stitches together

rep: repeat

RS: right side

sl1: slip one stitch from the left to the right needle without working it; all stitches in the projects are slipped purlwise

st(s): stitch(es)

tbl: through back of loop(s)

tog: together

WS: wrong side

* work instructions after asterisk(s) as directed

[ ] work instructions within square brackets as directed

WORKING FROM CHARTS

All of the charts in this book are worked in stocking (stockinette) stitch (knit on RS rows, purl on WS rows) unless indicated otherwise. A key is provided to explain different stitch instructions and show which yarn colours to use. Work each chart from the bottom upwards, reading all RS rows from right to left and all WS rows from left to right.

INTARSIA TECHNIQUE

Use the intarsia technique whenever a change of yarn colour is indicated on a chart. It is best to use a small ball or long length of yarn for each area of colour, otherwise the yarns will easily become tangled. When changing to a new colour, twist the yarns on the WS to prevent a hole from forming.

When starting a new row, turn the knitting so that the yarns that are hanging from it untwist as much as possible. If you have several colours, you may occasionally have to reorganize the yarns at the back of the knitting. Your work may look messy but once the ends are all sewn in it will look fine.

WRAP STITCH

Sometimes a pattern requires you to turn the work partway through a row. Working a wrap stitch avoids a hole from forming where the row is turned.

Wrapping a stitch on a knit row: Bring the yarn forward between the needles, slip a stitch purlwise from the left needle to the right needle, take the yarn back between the needles and then return the slipped stitch to the left needle.

Wrapping a stich on a purl row: Take the yarn back between the needles, slip a stitch purlwise from the left to the right needle, bring the yarn forward between the needles and then return the slipped stitch to the left needle.

Getting rid of a wrap stitch: When the turning rows have been completed, use this technique to disguise the loops that appear around the wrapped stitches. Work up to the wrap stitch and insert the right needle up through the front (on a knit row) or back (on a purl row) of the wrap. At the same time, put the needle through the stitch directly above the wrap and work the two together.

Love Crafts?

Keep updated on all exciting craft news from Collins & Brown

Register online at www.lovecrafts.co.uk for email updates on forthcoming titles

YARN SUPPLIERS
www.knitrowan.com
www.patonsyarns.com
www.coatscraft.co.uk

AUTHOR THANKS
Thanks to Coats Crafts for allowing me to use their wonderful yarns and for their continued support, in particular Sharon Brant and Kate Buller. Thanks to Katherine Lymer for her wonderful and very speedy knitting! A huge thank you to Jez for his love and support and his attention to architectural detail!

PICTURE CREDITS
Photography by Holly Jolliffe.
Illustrations by Marcus Butt.

ANSWERS TO QUIZ LONDON (P88)
1. Buckingham Palace, St James's Palace, Horse Guards Parade and Windsor Castle.
2. There are around 40,000 listed buildings in London.
3. They are: the Tower of London, Maritime Greenwich, Westminster Palace and the Royal Botanic Gardens at Kew.
4. The British Museum.